Need to Know
Epilepsy

Kristina Routh

Heinemann
LIBRARY

www.heinemann.co.uk/library
Visit our website to find out more information about **Heinemann Library** books.

To order:
☎ Phone 44 (0) 1865 888066
🗎 Send a fax to 44 (0) 1865 314091
💻 Visit the Heinemann Bookshop at www.heinemann.co.uk/library to browse our catalogue and order online.

Produced by Monkey Puzzle Media Ltd
Gissing's Farm, Fressingfield, Suffolk IP21 5SH, UK

First published in Great Britain by Heinemann Library, Halley Court, Jordan Hill, Oxford OX2 8EJ, part of Harcourt Education.
Heinemann is a registered trademark of Harcourt Education Ltd.

Editorial: Cath Senker
Design: Jane Hawkins
Picture Research: Sally Cole
Production: Viv Hichens

Originated by Ambassador Litho Ltd
Printed and bound in Hong Kong, China by
 South China Printing Company

ISBN 0 431 09763 1
08 07 06 05 04
10 9 8 7 6 5 4 3 2 1

The publishers would like to thank Shelley Wagstaff, Advice and Information Services Co-ordinator at Epilepsy Action, for her help in the preparation of the text, and the National Society for Epilepsy for their help in providing photos.

British Library Cataloguing in Publication Data
Routh, Kristina
 Epilepsy. – (Need to know)
 1.Epilepsy - Juvenile literature
 I.Title
 616.8'53

Acknowledgements
The publishers would like to thank the following for permission to reproduce photographs: AKG London p. 6; Alamy p. 18 (Nick Ayliffe); Corbis pp. 19 (DiMaggio/Kalish), 22 (José Luís Peleaz, Inc), 24 (Ariel Skelley), 34 (Mauro Panci), 37 (Frank Trapper), 39 (Joe Bator), 40 (Strauss/Curtis), 45 (José Luís Peleaz, Inc); Getty Images p. 51 (Taxi); Image State p. 32; Imaging Body pp. 1, 47; Mary Evans pp. 7, 8; Medic Alert p. 35; National Society for Epilepsy pp. 4, 13 (Ann D. Priest), 15, 30; Rex Features p. 26 (Julian Makey); Science Photo Library pp. 10 (BSIP Vem), 21 (John Greim), 28 (Custom Medical Stock Photo), 29 (John Greim), 31 (BSIP, LA/Filin Herrera), 33 (BSIP Collet), 46, 48 (Eye of Science), 49 (Robin Laurance); Support Dogs p. 17; Topham Picturepoint pp. 27 (Chapman), 42 (Image Works); Wellcome Trust Photo Library p. 12.

Cover photographs reproduced courtesy of Alamy/Alex Segre and the Epilepsy Society/Ann D. Priest.

Contents

Any words appearing in the text in bold, **like this**, are explained in the Glossary.

Introducing epilepsy

Epilepsy has been around for thousands of years, probably for the whole of human history. It is very common. The name 'epilepsy' comes from a Greek word meaning to be 'held' or 'seized'. **Epileptic seizures** are brief spells when the messages inside the brain get mixed up and people lose control of their bodies.

During a seizure people with epilepsy may lose control of their bodies and fall to the ground.

Anyone can have a seizure but people with epilepsy have seizures more than once. With epilepsy, seizures may happen just a few times, or over and over again.

They happen suddenly, often for no reason, then go away as quickly as they came. A seizure can involve blacking out (becoming unconscious) with the body going stiff and twitching. Alternatively, the person may experience abnormal movements or sensations, or just stare into space for a few seconds.

Whatever the type, seizures can cause a lot of problems for the person with epilepsy. Having seizures can be very uncomfortable and embarrassing, and the person may even get hurt. Most people with epilepsy take medicines to stop the seizures. No medicine can cure epilepsy but it can help those with epilepsy to live more normal lives.

Using the right words

When talking about people with any medical condition or disability it is important to use the right words. People with epilepsy are just that – people, like anyone else, who happen to have a condition called epilepsy. Sometimes the older name 'epileptic' is used to describe a person with epilepsy, but this can be hurtful. It gives the impression that the most important thing about that person is his or her medical condition.

Two other words that are no longer used are 'fit' and 'convulsion'. These days, the word 'seizure' is used to describe what happens, as it seems less negative.

Misunderstandings

Probably the greatest difficulty facing people with epilepsy is not the seizures themselves, but the attitude of some other people. Many people do not understand seizures, so they are scared or suspicious of people who have them. A lot of work is being done to teach members of the public about epilepsy so that they will be able to understand, accept and help the people who live with it.

"Strange and absurd thoughts run through my mind. Then I feel the seizure flood through me like a wave and all of my muscles tighten. As my throat tightens I can't speak or say anything; all I can do is breathe out so I seem to make a quiet, deep screaming sound."

(Barry, aged 25, UK)

History

Throughout history, epilepsy has often been misunderstood. Believed to be suffering a kind of madness, people with epilepsy have been feared, pitied, punished and even locked away.

Despite this, some people in the past who had epilepsy led successful lives, some becoming world leaders. Julius Caesar had epilepsy yet he ruled the Roman Empire. Napoleon Bonaparte did not let his epilepsy stop him from leading France to victory on the battlefields. It is thought that even Alexander the Great, who conquered much of the known world for the Greeks, may have had epilepsy.

The ancient world

Epilepsy has been fascinating people for thousands of years. Indian writings from 2000 BCE describe **seizures**. There are ancient Babylonian tablets in the British Museum that tell of the condition.

Ancient peoples such as the Romans and the Greeks knew about epilepsy but they believed it was due to **supernatural** forces, usually evil ones. Some thought epilepsy was a sacred (holy) disease, sent by the gods. Many of their treatments were based on spiritual or religious ceremonies.

Napoleon Bonaparte, the powerful French emperor, had epilepsy.

Even in ancient times, though, some people got it right. One of these was Hippocrates, sometimes called the Father of Medicine. He lived in ancient Greece around 400 BCE. He believed epilepsy was a disorder of the brain and had absolutely nothing to do with either gods or evil spirits.

Middle Ages

During the Middle Ages in Europe most people were ignorant about epilepsy. For hundreds of years it was again believed to be due to possession by evil spirits, or devils. People with epilepsy were treated with fear and suspicion.

Epilepsy was sometimes known as the 'falling sickness' and was often treated by prayer or fasting (going without food). Another treatment was exorcism – a ceremony in which so-called evil spirits were driven out using prayers or magic. People with epilepsy often prayed to the saints to help them, the most popular being St Valentine, who became the patron saint of epilepsy. None of these treatments cured the condition.

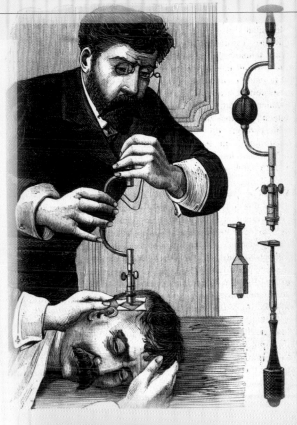

Trepanation – drilling a hole in the skull – was once thought to relieve epilepsy by letting out evil spirits.

Treatments for epilepsy

People thought they could cure epilepsy in all sorts of crazy ways. One gruesome treatment involved scraping the inside of the skull of a dead person and eating the scrapings over a period of several months. Another was drilling a hole in the head of the person with epilepsy. This was supposed to let out the evil spirits.

Into modern times

In the late 19th century, doctors and scientists throughout Europe and in the USA began to study people with epilepsy more closely. They realized that epilepsy was a disorder of the brain. This meant that there might be medicines that could treat epilepsy, just like there were for other diseases and conditions.

New medicines

The first proper medicines for epilepsy were bromides, which were first used in 1857. Sir Charles Locock, an English doctor, noticed that they seemed to reduce seizures in some patients. Other medicines came in later, such as phenobarbitone in 1912 and phenytoin in 1938. Phenytoin is an effective medicine still used today. Since the 1960s many new medicines for epilepsy have been introduced. Today around 80 per cent of people with epilepsy can be helped by medicines if they live in a place where medicines are available.

New techniques

In the 1920s a man called Hans Berger in Germany developed a new test called the **electroencephalogram**, or EEG. This involved recording the electrical activity of the brain and it was soon being used to test for epilepsy. EEGs could help find the part of the brain that was affected by seizures. This led to the introduction of surgery for epilepsy in the 1950s.

An EEG machine in New York, USA, in 1964, being used to study the brain's electrical activity during dreaming.

In recent years, testing for epilepsy has been helped by the invention of new types of **scanners** that can observe the brain from the outside. New treatments such as **vagal nerve stimulation** have been developed (see page 32). More and more research is being done to try to understand and to treat epilepsy.

Changes in attitude

Just as important for the person with epilepsy is the change in attitude of other people over the years. Where once people with epilepsy were feared and excluded, sometimes even imprisoned, now there is more understanding. Although there is still **prejudice** against those who have this condition, attitudes are slowly improving. New laws have been passed in many countries to make sure that people with conditions like epilepsy are not treated unfairly at work. In addition, organizations such as Epilepsy Action in the UK and the Epilepsy Foundation in the USA are helping to educate people about epilepsy and dispel the many myths surrounding it.

What is epilepsy?

Epilepsy is a serious medical condition but it is not a disease and it cannot be caught from someone else. Most people who have epilepsy are just like everyone else except that from time to time they have a brief disturbance of the brain called a **seizure**.

What is a seizure?

The brain is made up of a mass of cells, called **neurons**, which connect to each other in very complicated ways. Electrical messages are constantly being passed from one neuron to another and down nerves to the muscles in the body.

A seizure happens when there is a sudden, unexpected storm of electrical activity in the brain. No one really knows exactly why this happens. The neurons in one area of the brain just have a tendency to 'fire off' faster than usual from time to time. This abnormal activity spreads to the surrounding neurons, sometimes affecting the whole brain. This means that the electrical messages between cells get mixed up and so the muscles may stop

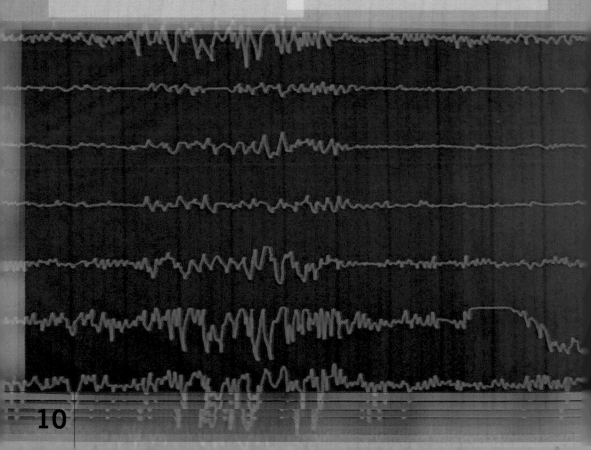

working or work too hard for a while. When the seizure passes after a few seconds or minutes the brain returns to normal.

For some people with epilepsy these seizures happen every day. For some they may happen only once or twice a year. Epilepsy cannot be cured but in many cases will eventually go away on its own. No one really knows why.

Here an electroencephalograph makes a tracing of brainwaves during a seizure.

Types of seizure

There are over 40 different types of seizure and each person's is slightly different. But there are a few common types. **Generalized seizures** affect the whole brain. **Partial seizures** affect a small part of the brain.

What happens to the body during a seizure depends upon the part of the brain affected and how much it is affected. In the best-known kind of **epileptic** seizure, the person falls to the floor unconscious, with arms and legs jerking. Other types may involve movement in just a small part of the body, like an arm or leg.

In some seizures there is no movement at all and the person just appears to be daydreaming. For others there may be strange feelings, and they may even sense smells that do not exist.

When are seizures not epilepsy?

There are some things that can make most people's brains have a seizure, such as very high temperatures (especially in young children) and some medicines. A person may have one seizure and never have another. Doctors only say a person has epilepsy when he or she has had more than one seizure, and other illnesses have been ruled out.

11

Whole brain seizures

When the burst of unusual electrical activity affects the whole or nearly all of the brain, it is called a **generalized seizure**. The most common types of generalized **seizure** are **tonic-clonic seizures** and **absence seizures**.

Tonic-clonic seizure

The old-fashioned name for a tonic-clonic seizure is a **grand mal** seizure. It is what most people imagine when they think of epilepsy. The person having the seizure loses consciousness and so is unaware of what is happening. The individual falls to the ground and the muscles contract and go stiff. He or she may seem to cry out as the chest muscles push air out of the lungs, and the lips may turn blue. Sometimes the person wets him or herself because of losing control of the bladder muscles. The seizure normally lasts only a few minutes and then the body relaxes. Many people recover quickly, but for some it may take hours or even days for them to feel completely better.

Absence seizure

Absence seizures occur most often in children. Although they lose consciousness there are no abnormal movements of the body. In fact, a person can have an absence seizure without anyone noticing! He or she may just seem to be daydreaming and will not answer if spoken to. These used to be called **petit mal** seizures.

Absence seizures usually last only a few seconds and then the person will 'wake up'. He or she may not even realize that a seizure has occurred. These seizures can cause problems in school because the child may miss important things in the lesson or the teacher may think the child is deliberately not paying attention.

During a tonic-clonic seizure a person may have foam around the mouth because saliva cannot be swallowed.

12

> **"Have you ever been sitting in class and just totally spaced out? I have! Finally my mom took me to the doctor and he found out I was having absence seizures."**
>
> (Katie, aged 18, Epilepsy Foundation, USA)

First aid

It is important for family, friends and workmates to know how to help a person who has tonic-clonic seizures:

- Never hold the person down.
- Remove harmful objects or furniture.
- Put something soft under the head.
- Don't put anything in the mouth.
- Place the individual in the recovery position (lying on his or her side) afterwards in case he or she is sick.
- Stay with the person to calm and reassure him or her.
- Call for medical help if the seizure lasts for longer than five minutes, if another attack starts right away or if the person has injured him or herself.

After a seizure the person should be placed in the recovery position and given reassurance.

13

Partial seizures

In a **partial seizure**, only part of the brain is affected by abnormal electrical activity. Over half of the people who have epilepsy get this type of seizure. It can vary greatly from person to person.

Simple partial seizures

A **simple partial seizure** is when a small part of the brain is affected and the person stays conscious. What happens will depend upon the area of the brain affected. There may be twitching of muscles, strange emotions and feelings, or sensing unpleasant tastes and smells. The person may feel sweaty and sick.

During the seizure, which usually only lasts for a few seconds, the person will be aware of what is happening and this can be quite upsetting. Sometimes a **generalized seizure** follows afterwards. If so, the partial seizure can act as a warning to the person. This warning symptom is sometimes called an **aura**.

Complex partial seizures

Sometimes a larger area of the brain is affected and the person may go into a dreamlike state. He or she seems to be awake but cannot respond to people. This is called a **complex partial seizure**.

People may appear to behave quite strangely during the seizure. They may pull at their clothes, mumble, walk around as if they are drunk or smack their lips and swallow over and over again. They may cry out and appear confused. Anything that can happen during a simple partial seizure can also happen during this type of seizure, but the person will probably not remember it.

This type of epilepsy is sometimes named after the area of the brain involved. **Temporal lobe epilepsy** is a well-known example. The temporal lobes are the areas in each half of the brain that lie at the sides above the ears. They have many functions, which include feeling emotions and receiving information about smell. They are also involved in memory.

Someone having a partial seizure may appear to act strangely. Onlookers can help by speaking calmly to him or her.

Strange behaviour

A person having a partial seizure can seem to be acting very strangely. Often onlookers do not know about this type of epilepsy and so do not understand what is happening. They may even think that the person is drunk. The person having the seizure needs gentle reassurance until the seizure has passed and he or she has recovered.

Inside a seizure

There are so many different kinds of **seizure** that almost everyone will have a different story to tell about how they feel. Some people will be wide awake while their body twitches or moves on its own. Some people feel as though they are dreaming, or even drunk, during the seizure. They may even have déjà vu, an odd experience where a person feels they have been in exactly the same situation before.

If the whole brain is affected, the person having a seizure will be unconscious and not aware of anything at all. The individual may get hurt or wet him or herself and not know it. Afterwards the person usually feels confused and very sleepy.

Seizure alert dogs

Many people with epilepsy believe their pet dogs can predict their seizures. They say their dog has come running to them just before their seizure starts. Amazingly, it seems that these stories are true. These pets pick up some sort of signal from their owners. As the dogs often come running in from another room, this signal is possibly a special 'seizure odour'.

Lizzy describes her seizures

Lizzy is a 21-year-old secretary in the UK, who was diagnosed with epilepsy at 19. 'Nearly all the time I know if I am going to have a seizure. My heart beats faster, my hands start shaking, my brain tells my hands to do something but nothing happens. To people around me it looks like I'm daydreaming. Then my hands clench and my muscles start to spasm. After that it's just nothing until I hear voices when I come round. After the seizure it's headache, tiredness, bruises, cuts, sore tongue, aching jaw and just having no energy in my body to do anything.'

Perhaps the dogs can smell an odour given off by their owner's body.

It is hard to train dogs to react like this – to become **seizure alert dogs**. It is much easier to train dogs to help their owners after a seizure has started. **Seizure response dogs** can go and get help from a family member, help their owner get up off the floor or just stay by their owner's side to protect him or her.

> **"Before I had my dog I had a lot of epilepsy and a little life; now I have a little epilepsy and a lot of life."**

(A happy seizure alert dog owner, via Dr T. Betts, Queen Elizabeth Psychiatric Hospital, Birmingham, UK)

Seizure alert dogs form a strong bond with their owners.

What can trigger a seizure?

Seizures usually happen quite out of the blue but there are some things that can set them off. These are known as **triggers**. People with epilepsy soon learn what can trigger their seizures and try to avoid these situations. Some triggers, such as alcohol and certain medicines, can cause seizures even in people who do not have epilepsy.

Lack of sleep

Tiredness is one of the most common and most significant triggers in epilepsy. Missing sleep, or a change in sleeping pattern, can bring on seizures. This can be a problem for teenagers who want to stay out late with friends or do schoolwork late at night.

Alcohol

Too much alcohol can trigger a seizure. If people with epilepsy drink alcohol, it is best to drink only a little, as it can interfere with the medicines they take.

Flashing lights can cause seizures in people with photosensitive epilepsy (see page 19).

❝I felt devastated when I had another seizure but realized that it was brought on by worrying about my exams, staying up late and drinking two glasses of wine.❞

(Sandra, aged 17, from Epilepsy Association, Australia)

Stress

Stress and worry are known to trigger seizures in some people with epilepsy. Stress seems to cause the **neurons** in the brain to become 'over-excitable' and make a seizure more likely to happen. Being worried can also keep people awake when they should be sleeping at night, or they might forget to take their medication. In both these cases, a seizure may be triggered. It is hard to avoid stress and worry but there are ways that people can be taught to cope with them.

Drugs

People with epilepsy who take illegal drugs increase their chances of having a seizure. Some drugs, like cocaine, can actually cause seizures. All drug-taking tends to upset an individual's lifestyle and routine. The person may not eat properly or get enough sleep. All these things can make seizures more likely.

Photosensitivity

Some people with epilepsy have a condition called **photosensitivity**. Certain things they see, such as flashing lights, can trigger seizures. They may have problems watching TV, dancing in a club that has strobe lights, or even using a computer monitor – although this is rare. A few individuals may have seizures when they see patterns of dark and light stripes. Computer and video games often have warnings about photosensitivity and advise that people with this type of epilepsy should be extremely careful when they play.

Are seizures harmful?

Seizures may be unpleasant for the person with epilepsy, and worrying for those who see them, but they are not usually harmful. Many people with epilepsy live long, active lives even though they may have seizures from time to time. Some do die earlier than expected but this is usually because of other diseases, or as a result of injuries and accidents that happen during a seizure.

During a **tonic-clonic seizure** a person loses control over his or her body. The person drops to the floor and may hit his or her head, or another part of the body. People may strike themselves on sharp edges of furniture as the muscles of their arms and legs contract and cause their limbs to jerk. The muscles of the jaw will clench, which may mean that they bite their tongue or the inside of the cheeks. Other dangers may arise from the situation in which the seizure takes place, such as when the person is in the bath, crossing the road or driving a car. It is up to bystanders to help protect the individual if they can.

Even though seizures themselves are not usually harmful, every person with epilepsy should know about two very serious situations called **status epilepticus** and **Sudden Unexpected Death in Epilepsy (SUDEP)**.

Status epilepticus

'Status epilepticus' means 'having continuous or repeated seizures'. This is a serious, life-threatening condition in which the seizure lasts much longer than normal, or where one seizure leads straight into another. Doctors do not quite agree on exactly how long a seizure has to last to be status epilepticus. Some say five minutes, some say ten, some longer. Yet they are all agreed that the condition should be treated immediately in a hospital with special medicines (to stop the seizures) and oxygen (because the seizures affect the person's breathing). In some cases, where a person has repeated bouts of status epilepticus, their carer might be trained how to treat them at home using special medicines placed into the mouth or **rectum**.

Doctors may find it hard to tell people with epilepsy about the risks of status epilepticus and SUDEP. But some families of people who have died from them have been very angry that they were never warned this might happen.

Sudden Unexected Death in Epilepsy

A few people with epilepsy die suddenly, for no apparent reason. This is called Sudden Unexpected Death in Epilepsy (SUDEP). It seems there may be an upset to the heart or lungs so that breathing stops and blood is not pumped around the body. It is thought that this type of death often follows shortly after the end of a seizure. Doctors are trying to work out whether there is a link to the medicines that the person has been taking for their epilepsy.

It used to be thought that SUDEP was very rare, but some studies have shown that it may happen in 8 to 17 per cent of people with epilepsy. SUDEP is very unusual in children but seems to be more common between the ages of 20 and 40.

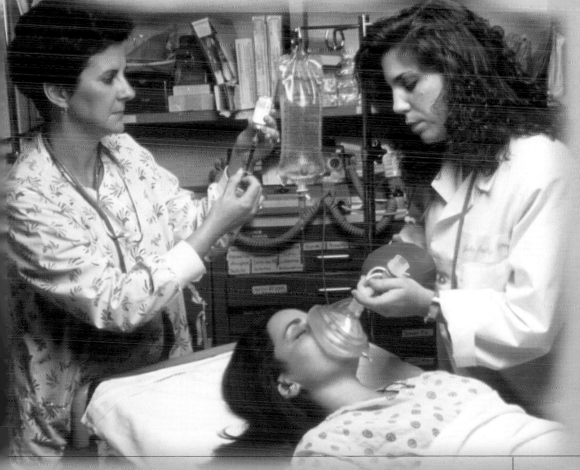

How common is epilepsy?

Because of worries about how they will be treated, many people with epilepsy do not talk about it. Most people are surprised to hear that epilepsy is actually very common.

In developed countries such as the USA, the United Kingdom, Australia and New Zealand, about 1 in 133 people have epilepsy. That may not sound like many, but in a school of 1000 students, 7 or 8 of them may have epilepsy. New cases of epilepsy are being diagnosed all the time. For instance, there are 120,000 new cases every year in a large country like the USA.

The reason epilepsy is so common is that it can affect so many different types of people. Epilepsy can affect people of all ethnic groups, in any part of the world. And both sexes can get epilepsy, although it may be slightly more common in males – no one really knows why.

Age and epilepsy

People of all ages can get epilepsy. However, most new cases are found in two particular age groups. These are children and young people under the age of 20, and older people over the age of 60. Many children who are diagnosed with epilepsy grow out of it as they become adults, for reasons that are not clear. Yet some will live with the condition all their lives.

Epilepsy worldwide

Epilepsy is a truly international condition. It is more common in some developing countries because people there are more likely to suffer from poor health. Brain infections, problems during childbirth and poor nutrition are all more likely in these countries and these can lead to epilepsy.

One big difference across the world is in the way epilepsy is treated. People with epilepsy in poorer, developing countries may not be able to afford the daily medicines they need to control their **seizures**. About three-quarters of all the people in the world with epilepsy go without proper medicines.

❝Epilepsy is the most common serious brain disorder. It affects at least 50 million people worldwide, 85 per cent of them living in developing countries.❞

(The World Health Organization)

People of all ages can get epilepsy. However, it is most likely to develop in children and in people over 60.

23

How common is epilepsy?

Anyone can get epilepsy

Scientists who study the human brain think that **seizures** can happen to anyone under certain circumstances. Some of those who get epilepsy probably have what is called a low '**seizure threshold**', which means that they are more likely to get seizures than others.

Many different causes

Epilepsy is not like measles or chicken pox, which have only one cause. Epilepsy has many causes, which include:

- Birth or development problems. Sometimes a baby's brain does not grow properly, or is damaged by an infection or lack of oxygen before it is born. Sometimes there is a problem during the birth itself. Such children may then have many problems, just one of which is epilepsy.

- Infection. When the brain or the surrounding tissues get infected (usually with bacteria or viruses), this can lead to seizures. These may then keep happening even after the infection has gone away. Perhaps the best-known example of a disease that can lead to epilepsy is **meningitis**.

- Head injuries. If someone's brain is damaged by a fall or by a knock to the head, the person may later develop epilepsy.

In over half of cases, the cause of epilepsy is unknown.

- Other illnesses. Any condition that affects the brain might cause seizures. Two of the most common are **strokes**, where the blood supply to part of the brain is cut off, and brain **tumours**, where a growth forms inside the brain. Epilepsy caused by these conditions is more common in older people.

- Genetic factors. In some cases epilepsy runs in families – **genes** (passed on from parents) may be involved. It seems that their genes give wrong instructions to the brain cells about how to link with each other. This may lead to the mixed-up electrical messages that cause seizures. In rare cases epilepsy is thought to be directly caused by one gene, or group of genes. Generally the genes make a person more likely to have a low seizure threshold.

Cause unknown

Over half the cases of epilepsy are known as idiopathic. This is simply a medical term for saying that no one knows what causes them! As more research is done, doctors may be able to discover why these people get epilepsy.

Brain injuries

The brain is very fragile. Anything that damages it may lead to epilepsy. After an injury or an illness the brain tries to repair itself but sometimes gets it wrong. It mixes up the 'wiring' a bit, making odd connections between **neurons** in the brain. This can cause the unusual electrical messages that occur in the brain during **seizures**.

The brain is protected by the skull, which acts like a crash helmet. It can still be damaged, though, if the head is hit very hard. This kind of injury can happen in a car crash, or if someone falls to the ground from a high place. The brain may be torn by a piece of broken skull bone, or squashed by a build-up of blood.

Rik Mayall

Rik Mayall, the British comedy actor, is probably best known for his outrageous performances in a cult comedy called 'The Young Ones'. Less well known is the fact that he has been taking medicine for epilepsy since 1998, when he suffered a near-fatal quad bike accident at his home. His brain had been damaged, which made him have seizures.

Rik says, 'I was supposed to take pills for a year until I knew it was safe, but I took them until Christmas and I got a bit bored.' (*Daily Telegraph*, UK, 29 July 1999.) After stopping his tablets he had another seizure, and bit his tongue badly. This convinced him that he should be more sensible and take his medication regularly. He now admits it 'could have been a lot worse'.

Bicycle helmets

Every year many children are taken to a hospital emergency department after falling off their bicycles and hitting their heads. Sadly, some of these children suffer brain damage, and a few even die. For some there will be many years of treatment for epilepsy ahead of them.

Wearing a good bicycle helmet cuts the risk of brain damage enormously. Helmets work by acting as shock absorbers – they cushion the skull. Some people may think that wearing protective headgear is not cool, but it is a lot better than risking brain damage, epilepsy and even death.

A bicycle helmet should fit the head snugly and the straps should be tight for cycling.

Epilepsy in the elderly

Many people are surprised to learn that a large number of the new cases of epilepsy each year occur among older people. Sometimes epilepsy is caused by other conditions and illnesses that are more common in older people.

Stroke

A **stroke** happens when an artery bringing blood to part of the brain gets too narrow or clogs up. The blood cannot get through properly and so a part of the brain loses its supply of oxygen. This damages the brain and can lead to seizures. About one in ten people who have a stroke will later have epilepsy.

Disease

There are brain diseases that affect the elderly in particular, and some of these may cause epilepsy. One is **Alzheimer's disease**, which causes changes in the structure of the brain with gradual loss of brain cells. People with Alzheimer's may have a poor memory and find it hard to perform simple everyday tasks. Diseases of other parts of the body, such as the kidney or liver, may also affect the brain and cause epilepsy in some people.

Older people are more likely to be affected by epilepsy.

Special care needed

Epilepsy in older people tends to be a little more difficult to deal with than in younger people. Sometimes it can be quite hard to tell if an elderly person has epilepsy because the seizures may not be very obvious. The person may just seem to be in a confused state, which could be caused by other things, such as the **side effects** of medication they are taking. An **EEG** test may be needed in order to diagnose epilepsy.

The medicines used to treat epilepsy (see page 30) can have strong side effects, even in young, fit people. In elderly people, the side effects may be worse. Also, older people are more likely to be taking other medicines already, and these may react with the epilepsy medicines.

Falls and confusion during seizures are often more serious in the elderly and there may be more frequent visits to the hospital. There are lots of different kinds of alarms and safety equipment that they can use in the home. Many elderly people cope well with epilepsy but some are not able to live alone without help from other people.

Wearing an alarm means this man can press a button to call for help if he falls.

Treatment

As yet, there is no cure for epilepsy but there are medicines that can usually stop **seizures** from happening. Four out of five people with epilepsy in developed countries find that taking medicine allows them to lead fairly normal lives without too many seizures.

Choosing the right medicine

There are around twenty different types of medicines for epilepsy. When a person first has epilepsy his or her doctor will choose a suitable medicine. The choice will depend upon the type of seizure the person gets and also his or her age, lifestyle, and how often the seizures occur. It also depends on whether the person is male or female.

It may take a while to get the correct dose of medicine. Too little and seizures might happen, too much and there might be bad **side effects** from the medicine. Usually people with epilepsy are given just one medicine but sometimes they may need to take two or more different types.

What are they called?

Some medicines that have been used for a long time are phenytoin, sodium valproate and carbamazepine. Newer ones include lamotrigine, topiramate and levetiracetam.

The various medicines used to treat epilepsy may have different names in different countries.

These are the **generic** or scientific names for the medicines. Each also has at least one **brand name** (rather like cola-flavoured drinks have brand names such as Coca-Cola and Pepsi). The same medicine can have different brand names in different countries.

Side effects

Side effects are the unwanted and sometimes harmful effects that all medicines can have on the human body. Many people have no side effects at all from their epilepsy medicines. But some feel sick, become drowsy or get a skin rash. These side effects are usually worst when the medicines are just being started or the dose is being changed. Things usually settle down as the person's body gets used to the medicine.

Stopping medicine

People with epilepsy who continue to have seizures need to keep taking medicine. Many people can stop taking their medicine if they have had no seizures for a long time – some doctors say two years, some say five. But no one should stop taking the medicines suddenly; they need to be stopped gradually under the supervision of a doctor.

Treatment

Other treatments

Most people with epilepsy take medicines that keep their seizures under control. For around one out of five people, medicines do not work very well and they still get a lot of seizures. Doctors might then try some other kinds of treatment.

Surgery

Surgery involves cutting into the skull to operate directly on the brain. Surgery on the brain can be difficult and risky so it is only used when other treatments fail. The person with epilepsy will have lots of tests before the operation to show which area of the brain is affected. Sometimes surgery works well, and the person gets fewer seizures or no more at all. But in other cases the seizures continue.

A child on the ketogenic diet can only eat sweet treats rarely.

Vagal nerve stimulation

Vagal nerve stimulation is a quite new way of treating epilepsy. A special battery is placed under the skin of the chest during an operation. This sends a regular pulse of electricity to the brain through a big nerve in the neck called the vagus. This pulse stops a seizure happening. The procedure does not cause any harm to the brain, which is used to receiving natural electrical impulses from the nerves.

Over 12,000 people with epilepsy around the world have now been treated in this way. For up to 50 per cent of the people treated, vagal nerve stimulation seems to reduce their seizures by one half. A few people become completely free of seizures.

The ketogenic diet

The **ketogenic diet** is sometimes used for children who get lots of seizures despite taking medicine. It is rich in fatty foods like cream and butter, but low in carbohydrates found in foods such as bread and cereal. The diet changes the way the body gets energy from food. For some children this treatment is successful in stopping seizures, but sometimes it does not work at all. No one really knows why.

Complementary therapy

Complementary therapies are based on different scientific ideas from the treatments offered by most doctors and hospitals. Some complementary therapies are useful in treating epilepsy but none of them can cure it.

Epilepsy around the world

In many countries good medical care is not easily available. Across the world, many people with epilepsy get no treatment at all and face real problems in their daily lives. The Global Campaign Against Epilepsy was started in 1997 by the World Health Organization and other international organizations to improve prevention, treatment, care and services around the world for people with epilepsy.

The ones that seem to work best are those that help the person with epilepsy to relax and become calmer, such as **aromatherapy** and, occasionally, hypnotherapy. It is important for people with epilepsy to continue to take their epilepsy medicines while using complementary therapies.

Some complementary therapies, such as aromatherapy, may help people with epilepsy by encouraging them to relax.

Everyday life

With the help of medicines, most people with epilepsy can lead fairly normal lives. They will probably try to avoid activities that might **trigger seizures** but will not let their epilepsy rule their lives.

Many of the problems met by people with epilepsy are caused by other people's attitudes to their condition. Throughout history, people with epilepsy have been labelled as sick, or even mad. This misunderstanding from other people, as well as the seizures themselves, can lead to many worrying questions for the person with epilepsy. Who should I tell about my condition? What about romance – will my partner still like me? Should I tell the truth in a job interview?

People with epilepsy should avoid carrying hot pans, like this.

Sometimes these worries can lead to poor self-esteem, depression and even suicide. It is thought that around one-third of people with epilepsy suffer from depression to some extent. For some people with epilepsy the worry about their condition may mean that they find it hard to face new people and new situations. They can become quite isolated.

However, doctors can often treat depression very successfully. With some help, most people with epilepsy do manage to cope and are able to lead full, happy lives.

Keeping safe

There are many things that people with epilepsy can do to help keep themselves safe if they have a seizure, such as:

- having a shower, not a bath (to reduce the risk of drowning if a seizure occurs), and keeping the door unlocked
- not bathing while alone at home
- not carrying hot pans when cooking
- avoiding free-standing heaters, and using sturdy fireguards
- fitting tough safety glass in low windows and doors
- padding sharp edges on furniture
- carrying a personal alarm.

Alert identification

It can be worrying if someone with epilepsy has a seizure while he or she is away from home. The person may be taken to hospital where it can be difficult for the doctors to tell what is wrong straight away. This is why some people choose to carry identification which states that they have epilepsy.

In many countries, people with epilepsy can join an organization that helps them with this identification. For a fee their details are put onto a computer, and they are given a card with a special telephone number. They also wear an eye-catching metal pendant or bracelet with a special picture and phone number on it.

This is a range of bracelets from Medic Alert, one of the best-known identification systems, which operates in the USA, UK, Australia and New Zealand.

Everyday life

Danny Glover's story

There are not many famous film actors who would stand up in front of thousands of people and tell them that they had epilepsy. But this is what Danny Glover did at the main Epilepsy Foundation meeting in 2001 in the USA. Best known for his roles in action films such as *Lethal Weapon*, Danny Glover has been an actor for many years.

Danny told the audience that he started having **seizures** when he was 15, and these had gone on until he was about 35. Then, for some reason, they stopped. The seizures had been very difficult to cope with – on one family trip he had six in a row. Later, when he became a stage actor, Danny was always worried that he might have a seizure on stage where everyone could see.

Because of his experiences with epilepsy, Danny wanted to support the work of the American Epilepsy Foundation, which helps people with epilepsy. He was especially interested in the organization's work with teenagers. Danny knew what it was like to be a teenager with epilepsy, trying to cope with having seizures as well as the usual challenges young people face.

Self-esteem

Danny talked about how important it is for young people with epilepsy to build up their self-esteem. Many people with epilepsy find it hard to believe in themselves. Sometimes this is made worse by the way other people treat them. It is difficult to respect yourself when other people treat you badly.

With the help of his parents Danny learnt to cope. At the Epilepsy Foundation meeting he said, 'I felt good about myself. I felt that I could accomplish something. Despite the fact that I had epilepsy, I felt that I could win.'

Where are the others?

It was a brave thing for Danny Glover to stand up and talk about his experiences with epilepsy. Given how common epilepsy is, there must be lots of other famous people who have it. Many are quite happy to talk about having other common conditions like diabetes or asthma but very few will admit to having epilepsy. One day, perhaps, there will be less fear and suspicion surrounding epilepsy. Then more people can be as open as Danny has been.

Danny Glover (right) with his *Lethal Weapon* co-star, Mel Gibson. Danny had epilepsy for twenty years and now supports the work of the Epilepsy Foundation in the USA.

Driving

If someone has a **seizure** while driving a car he or she will lose control of it and there could be a serious accident. So there are laws in most countries about driving and epilepsy. These laws vary from country to country and sometimes between regions. Every person who has epilepsy needs to find out what the laws are in his or her particular area.

In most places the law says that when someone has a seizure the person must tell the authorities that issue driving licences. The individual must then stop driving until he or she has gone for a certain length of time without having another seizure. This is usually one year. After that time the person will be allowed to drive again.

In most countries people with epilepsy are not permitted to drive public service vehicles, such as buses, unless they have not had any seizures for many years.

Facing disappointment

Most adults who develop epilepsy are disappointed when they have to stop driving. It may make it difficult for them to carry on with their normal lives. It is up to the person with epilepsy to be truthful about the seizures and it might be tempting to keep quiet and say nothing. But most people with epilepsy realize that they must think about the safety of others. They accept the fact that it is best that they do not drive while they might have a seizure.

"When I was having seizures they affected my driving a great deal – I managed to wreck two cars because I chose to drive when I felt like it."

(Estelle, Washington DC, USA, from the Epilepsy Foundation website)

Things to remember

There are a few extra things that people with epilepsy who can drive need to think about:

- Medicines for epilepsy can make alcohol seem stronger and so they should never drink at all before driving.
- Driving when tired can **trigger** seizures so they should always take regular breaks.
- If they are changing their epilepsy medicines they should not drive for a while in case the change of medicine results in seizures.
- It is a good idea to have some 'refresher' driving lessons if they are starting to drive again after a long break.
- People who develop epilepsy should check that their car insurance policy still covers them.

Sport and recreation

"Thinking ahead will often reduce the risk, relieve the fear and allow the person to enjoy their sport."

(Lorne Hyde, Epilepsy Association, Australia)

It is good for people with epilepsy to be involved in sport and other physical activities. The more healthy and active they are, the less likely they are to have **seizures**. Most sports can be enjoyed by people with epilepsy, especially if they take a few sensible steps to keep themselves safe.

People with epilepsy are all different and the type of activities they can do will depend upon the type of seizures they get and how often they get them. Every sport or activity has some sort of risk. It is up to the individual to decide whether that risk is worth taking, and to make sure they would not put someone else in danger.

For some activities it is sensible to have someone else close by to help in case a seizure happens. This is especially important if water is involved or if there could be a fall, such as in horse riding or mountaineering.

Contact sports such as football and rugby can usually be played by people with epilepsy. Special headgear is often worn that will give extra protection. If the epilepsy was caused by a head injury in the first place then these kinds of sports may not be safe.

Players should check with their doctors if they are not sure.

Just too dangerous

There are some activities that are really just too dangerous for people with epilepsy who have seizures. Sports such as boxing and full-contact martial arts are ruled out. Scuba diving, parachuting, flying a plane and motor racing should also be avoided as a moment's loss of control could lead to a serious accident.

Water safety

Everyone should learn to swim for his or her own safety, and swimming is a good way to get enjoyable exercise. Most people with epilepsy can enjoy the water and keep themselves safe by following a few simple rules:

- Never swim alone and always have a friend within arm's reach.
- Make sure there is a lifeguard there who knows first aid for a seizure.
- Make sure someone in charge knows that the swimmer has epilepsy.
- Never swim if unwell or tired.
- Avoid getting too cold, thirsty or hungry.
- Avoid overcrowded situations.

Education and employment

People with epilepsy should have the same chances that everyone around them has. For children this means a normal school life; for older teenagers and adults this usually includes further education and a job or career.

School

Most schools will probably have at least one child with epilepsy. Generally, these children will be just like any others in the school, having lessons, enjoying playtimes and taking part in school activities. Many children explain epilepsy to their friends so that they know what to do to help if they see a **seizure** occurring.

Teachers can learn how to recognize a seizure and how to look after the child if one happens during school hours. It is good for the teacher to know if a child has **absence seizures** because the child might miss parts of the lesson without anyone realizing.

Higher education

Like everyone else, many people with epilepsy are able to go on to higher education in a college or university.

Often colleges have someone whose job it is to help out students with epilepsy or other medical conditions. Students with epilepsy should think about the type of seizures they have, and how often they have them, when planning what to study.

Going to college can often mean a busy new social life. A new student with epilepsy should remember that seizures can be **triggered** by lack of sleep, drinking alcohol and using drugs. It is good to get into a steady daily routine and try to stick to it.

Jobs

Most people with epilepsy are able to do a wide range of jobs. Some would like to work but cannot get a job because employers think they would not be able to cope. In many countries there are now laws to stop such **discrimination** (unfair treatment) against people with a disability or a medical condition like epilepsy.

Even so there are still some jobs that people with epilepsy are not usually able to do. Some of these jobs are those that involve potentially dangerous machinery. Others include the armed forces and any job that involves driving a public vehicle such as working for the police, fire service or ambulance service, or driving a bus or train.

❝❝I have had epilepsy all my life but accept what I am. I would like to say to all the kids who have epilepsy – keep living your lives to the fullest.❞❞

(Robin, aged 15, Epilepsy Circle of Support, USA)

Women and epilepsy

Epilepsy, and the medicines taken for it, can affect women in several ways.

Menstruation (periods)

Some women who have epilepsy notice that their **seizures** happen more at certain times of the month than others, and especially around the time of their period. This is probably because of the changing levels of **hormones** in their bodies during the monthly menstrual cycle. Treatment is available to help with this.

Contraception

Some epilepsy medicines can stop the contraceptive pill from working properly. They make the body use up the chemicals in the pill more quickly. So a woman with epilepsy may have to use special contraceptive pills or other methods. Her doctor can help her choose the right type of contraceptive.

Fertility

Fertility means being able to get pregnant. In general, women who are taking medicine for epilepsy are slightly less likely to get pregnant than other women. This is partly due to the epilepsy itself, and partly due to the medicines they take for the condition. But most women with epilepsy should have no problems starting a family.

Pregnancy

Most of the babies born to women with epilepsy are perfectly healthy. When every baby grows there is a risk that it will not develop properly. This risk is a little higher if the mother is taking medicines for epilepsy. (Other medicines, not just those for epilepsy, can cause similar problems.)

It is important for a woman with epilepsy to talk to her doctor before she tries to have a baby. Together they can prepare for the pregnancy, perhaps by changing the medicines she is using. For instance, while all women who are trying to become pregnant are advised to take folic acid (a vitamin), women with epilepsy may be advised to take a much higher dose and for a longer period.

Motherhood

Mothers get very tired when they are caring for a new baby. As tiredness can be a **trigger** for seizures, both parents will need to take advice on how to keep the child safe if a seizure happens.

There is nothing to stop a woman with epilepsy breast-feeding; it is very good for her and the baby. Only a small amount of the anti-epilepsy medicine she takes will be passed to the baby in her milk. This is not usually enough to cause problems.

EEGs and brain scans

There are some tests that may be helpful for people with epilepsy. They are carried out in hospitals, using rather sophisticated equipment, but they do not hurt at all.

Electroencephalogram (EEG)

The **electroencephalogram (EEG)** test, which takes about half an hour to do, is one of the most important tests for epilepsy. EEGs record **brainwaves**, the tiny electrical signals given off by the brain as it works. The EEG machine does not put any electricity into the brain so the test is quite safe.

Small pads called electrodes are fixed to the scalp with special glue, or held to the head by a rubber cap. The patient lies still while the recording is being taken, perhaps being asked to open and close their eyes at some point. Flashing lights may be used to check whether the person is affected by them. The machine produces a print-out of the brainwaves, which the doctor can look at to see whether it is likely that the person has epilepsy.

An EEG helps the doctor decide whether a person has epilepsy.

Scanning

Scanning is a way of looking inside the body from the outside without causing any harm. Scans are used in epilepsy to see if there are any areas of abnormal tissue such as scars from a head injury, or brain **tumours**, which could be causing the **seizures**. If there are, it may be possible to remove them by surgery.

The **scanners** most often used in epilepsy are computerized axial tomography (CAT) and magnetic resonance imaging (MRI) scanners. These both use computers to produce pictures that look like slices through the brain but they make these pictures in different ways:

- CAT scans use X-rays to produce pictures of the brain from different angles. Many doctors prefer to use other types of scan (such as MRI) if they are available since they can pick up information that a CAT scan cannot show.

- MRI scans have been introduced in the last twenty years and have been very helpful in epilepsy. The scanner has a powerful magnet inside it. Images are produced by changes in the magnetic field, which are then analysed by a computer. MRI scanning is thought to be safe for most people so is a good choice if it is available.

Scanners can be used to produce detailed pictures of the brain. The person having the scan must lie very still.

Medical research

All over the world, scientists and doctors are working to try and make things better for the millions of people who have epilepsy. They are trying to answer questions about its causes and are looking for new medicines and treatments.

Studying the causes

There are many different areas of research into the causes of epilepsy including:

- **neurotransmitters**. Many scientists are investigating the importance of neurotransmitters. These are chemicals that help to control the way in which **neurons** communicate with each other. They may well have an important role to play in causing **seizures**.

- **genetics**. Scientists know that **genes** are linked to some kinds of epilepsy. In recent years a lot of work has been carried out to try to find the genes responsible.
  Information from the International Human Genome Project, which has mapped out the genes possessed by human beings, is being used to help identify possible 'epilepsy genes'. One day this may lead to a new test for epilepsy, new treatments or even a cure.

Studying human chromosomes (the small shapes around the cell nucleus) may one day lead to new tests for epilepsy, and maybe even a cure.

New medicines

The ideal medicine for epilepsy would completely stop all seizures and produce no bad **side effects** at all. No such medicine exists yet, although there have been some very effective new drugs in recent years. Doctors and scientists are continually trying to produce new medicines for epilepsy. One research organization alone has tested 22,000 substances since 1975! Perhaps, one day, people with epilepsy will be able to take a pill each day and forget all about their condition.

Scientists are working hard to find new medicines for epilepsy.

Helping with research

Some people with epilepsy may be able to assist with research by offering to help test new medicines. This is important because, until a new medicine is actually used in a person with epilepsy, the doctors cannot tell if it works. People from families with several members who have epilepsy can help in genetic research. The scientists need to study these families to find out more about the genes that may be involved.

Epilepsy in the future

Epilepsy causes a lot of distress and suffering to millions of people across the world. And epilepsy is expensive. Many countries spend enormous amounts of money on health care for people with epilepsy, and every country loses out when so many of its people are affected.

Because of this, doctors and scientists will keep on fighting epilepsy. In the years to come they will find out more about the causes of epilepsy, find better medicines and treatments – and perhaps even discover a cure one day.

Accepting epilepsy

Many people with epilepsy have shown that they will not let their lives be spoiled by their condition. With the help of medicines and other treatments they control their **seizures** and make their own choices about how to live.

Perhaps the hardest thing about having epilepsy is the way other people treat those who have it.

To have seizures can be upsetting and embarrassing but to be feared and excluded is every bit as bad.

Things are slowly getting better. Laws have been passed in many countries that make it illegal to discriminate against people because of their medical condition. In recent years epilepsy has been discussed more freely in schools, in the media and on the Internet.

People with epilepsy are starting to feel happier about telling those around them about their condition.

One day, perhaps, epilepsy will be a thing of the past. Until then people with epilepsy need to be treated fairly, understood and accepted.

Picked on at school

Sue is a teenager living in Australia. When she was 14 she started getting **complex partial seizures**. She would seem to pick at her clothes and then fall to the floor, her body jerking. The other kids called her a 'freak' and her friends stopped inviting her to stay at weekends. Not surprisingly, she became isolated and depressed, falling behind in her schoolwork. Things became so bad that her parents decided to teach her at home until her seizures were controlled with medication. Her family then moved to another area so that she could have a fresh start at a new school.

❝We won't rest until we have achieved our goal: to live in a society where everyone understands epilepsy.❞

(Epilepsy Action, UK)

Information and advice

Many organizations offer information about living with epilepsy, and have helplines people can call for confidential information. Some have special sections to help teenagers and children who have epilepsy, or who would like to find out more about this condition. These organizations also play an important role in encouraging and supporting research into epilepsy.

Contacts in the UK

Epilepsy Action
New Anstey House
Gate Way Drive
Yeadon
Leeds LS19 7XY
Freephone Epilepsy Helpline: 0808 800 5050
Tel: 0113 210 8800
Fax: 0113 391 0300
Email helpline: helpline@epilepsy.org.uk
Email: epilepsy@epilepsy.org.uk
Website: www.epilepsy.org.uk
Epilepsy Action offers information about epilepsy and has a section for teenagers – 'upBEAT' – where young people can get advice by email or phone or join online discussion forums.

National Society for Epilepsy
Chesham Lane
Chalfont St Peter, Bucks SL9 0RJ
Tel: 01494 601300
Fax: 01494 871927
Helpline: 01494 601400 (10 a.m.–4 p.m., Monday to Friday)
Website: www.epilepsynse.org.uk

The NSE aims to provide information and raise awareness about epilepsy among people affected by epilepsy and among the general public. As well as running a helpine this organization supports research and provides residential care and rehabilitation for people with epilepsy.

Contacts in the USA

Epilepsy Foundation
4351 Garden City Drive
Landover, MD 20785-7223
Tel: (800) 332-1000
Website: www.efa.org
The Epilepsy Foundation provides information about epilepsy and support to those affected by it. 'Blurt' – the section of the website for teenagers – has stories about people with epilepsy, and offers discussion groups and chat rooms for young people with epilepsy.

Contacts in Australia

Epilepsy Association
To visit:
National Community Services Centre
Head Office, Suite 8 "Oxford Place"
44-46 Oxford Street
EPPING NSW 2121

Or send mail to:
GPO Box 9878
IN YOUR CAPITAL CITY
Tel: 1300 36 61 62
Fax: (02) 9869 4122
Email: epilepsy@epilepsy.org.au
Website: www.epilepsy.com.au

The Epilepsy Association offers information and support as well as running a range of activities for those with epilepsy. The website provides a section for teenagers with information about coping with epilepsy, and first aid. There is also a confidential helpline.

Contacts in New Zealand

Epilepsy New Zealand
PO Box 1074
Hamilton
Tel: (64) 7 834 3556
Fax: (64) 7 834 3553
Email: national@epilepsy.org.nz
Website: www.epilepsy.org.nz
Epilepsy New Zealand offers information about epilepsy and support via a national helpline. The organization also provides field officers – trained people who can go out to help those with epilepsy in their community.

Contacts worldwide

International League Against Epilepsy
Headquarters Office
Avenue Marcel Thiry 204, B-1200
Brussels, Belgium
Tel: + 32 (0) 2 774 9547
Fax: + 32 (0) 2 774 9690
Email: dsarliaux@ilae-epilepsy.org
Website: www.ilae-epilepsy.org
This is a global professional non-profit international organization. Together with the World Health Organization it has formed the 'Global Campaign against Epilepsy', which aims to improve the diagnosis, treatment, prevention and social acceptability of epilepsy.

Further reading

The Facts about Epilepsy, by Claire Llewellyn; Belitha Press, 2001. Examines the impact of the condition on daily life and practical measures needed to treat it.

The Illustrated Junior Encyclopedia of Epilepsy, edited by Dr Richard Appleton; Petroc Press, 1995. This encyclopedia is written for young people (9–14), and is aimed at helping them and their carers understand more about epilepsy.

Living with Epilepsy, by Patsy Westcott; Hodder Wayland, 1998. This book gives clear written and visual information about the condition in a factual and very easy-to-read format.

Taking Seizure Disorders to School, by Kim Gosslin; JayJo Books, 1996. This book for young people is designed to dispel myths about epilepsy. It fills the need to explain seizures to classmates of young people with epilepsy

Epilepsy: I Can Live With That, edited by Sue Goss; Epilepsy Foundation of Victoria, 1995. The experience of epilepsy as recorded by a group of ordinary men and women in Australia.

Disclaimer
All the Internet addresses (URLs) given in this book were valid at the time of going to press. However, due to the dynamic nature of the Internet, some addresses may have changed, or sites may have changed or ceased to exist since publication. While the author and Publisher regret any inconvenience this may cause readers, no responsibility for any such changes can be accepted by either the author or the Publisher.

Glossary

absence seizure
a type of seizure in which the person becomes unaware of their surroundings for a few seconds

Alzheimer's disease
a brain disease most commonly found in the elderly – changes in the structure of the brain cause loss of memory and make the person unable to think clearly

aromatherapy
a type of complementary therapy involving strong-smelling oils

aura
a warning symptom, such as a change in the sense of vision, hearing or even smell, that some people get before a full seizure

brainwaves
tiny electrical signals given off by the brain, which can be measured during an EEG test

brand name
the brand name of a medicine is what it is called by a particular company – one medicine can have several different brand names

complementary therapy
a treatment that does not use the same scientific ideas as the type of treatments offered by most doctors and hospitals, and is used alongside them

complex partial seizures
seizures affecting only part of the brain which, even so, cause a change in consciousness

discrimination
unfair treatment based, for example, on a person's colour, religion, ethnic group, gender or medical health

electroencephalogram (EEG)
a test that measures the electrical signals of the brain, which is used to help find out if a person has epilepsy

epileptic
used as a noun: an old fashioned word for someone with epilepsy that is no longer used – it can still be used as an adjective, for example, a person may be said to have 'epileptic seizures'

gene
a unit inside a cell that controls a particular quality in a living thing that has been passed on from its parents

generalized seizure
a seizure in which the whole brain is affected

generic name
the scientific or chemical name of a medicine – each medicine has only one generic name

genetics
the scientific study of the ways in which different features are passed down from parents to children

grand mal
an old-fashioned name for a tonic-clonic generalized seizure

hormones
chemical substances produced in the body that influence the way in which the cells and tissues function

ketogenic diet
special high-fat, low-carbohydrate diet sometimes used for children with epilepsy

meningitis
a dangerous infection of the coverings of the brain that can be caused by bacteria or viruses

neurons
cells of the nervous system, including brain cells

neurotransmitters
chemicals that help control how brain cells communicate with each other

partial seizure
a seizure that affects only part of the brain

petit mal
the old-fashioned name for absence seizures

photosensitivity
someone with photosensitivity may have their seizures triggered by flashing lights, TV screens or even stripes

prejudice
negative feelings towards a group of people that are not based on factual information

rectum
the end section of the tube through which solid waste leaves the body at the anus

scanners
machines that can take pictures of the inside of the body without harming it; the best known are computerized axial tomography (CAT) and magnetic resonance imaging (MRI) scanners

seizure
a sudden, unexpected 'storm' of electrical activity in the brain

seizure alert (or response) dogs
dogs that are trained to predict seizures or to help if a seizure happens

seizure threshold
an indication of how likely a person is to have a seizure; someone with a low seizure threshold will have seizures easily

side effects
the unwanted and sometimes harmful effects that all medicines can have on the body

simple partial seizures
seizures affecting only part of the brain; the person remains aware of what is happening

status epilepticus
a serious, life-threatening condition in which a seizure lasts much longer than normal, or where one seizure leads into another

stroke
damage to part of the brain caused by a lack of adequate blood supply

Sudden Unexpected Death in Epilepsy (SUDEP)
a few people with epilepsy die for no obvious reason, and this is called SUDEP

supernatural
something that cannot be explained by the laws of science

temporal lobe epilepsy
a well-known type of complex partial seizure

tonic-clonic seizure
a generalized seizure in which the person stiffens, loses consciousness, falls to the floor and their muscles jerk

trigger
something that can set off a seizure

tumour
abnormal overgrowth of the cells in any part of the body, usually forming a lump; it may be harmless, or cancerous and harmful

vagal nerve stimulation
a new treatment for epilepsy in which a pulse of electricity is sent up the vagal nerve (a big nerve in the neck) to the brain

Index

Titles in the *Need to Know* series include:

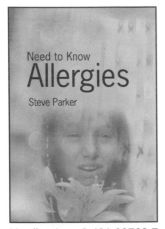

Need to Know
Allergies
Steve Parker

Hardback   0 431 09760 7

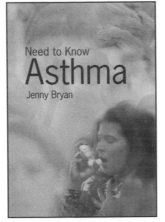

Need to Know
Asthma
Jenny Bryan

Hardback   0 431 09761 5

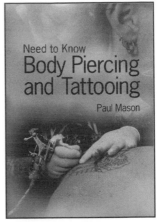

Need to Know
Body Piercing and Tattooing
Paul Mason

Hardback   0 431 09818 2

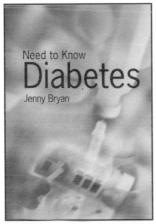

Need to Know
Diabetes
Jenny Bryan

Hardback   0 431 09762 3

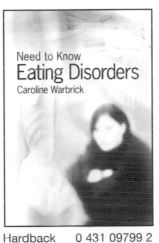

Need to Know
Eating Disorders
Caroline Warbrick

Hardback   0 431 09799 2

Need to Know
Epilepsy
Kristina Routh

Hardback   0 431 09763 1

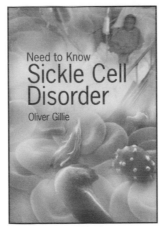

Need to Know
Multiple Sclerosis
Alexander Burnfield

Hardback   0 431 09764 X

Need to Know
Sickle Cell Disorder
Oliver Gillie

Hardback   0 431 09765 8

Need to Know
Teenage Sex
Caroline Carter

Hardback   0 431 09821 2

Find out about the other titles in this series on our website www.heinemann.co.uk/library